Ishy Din

Snookered

T0262506

B L O O M S B U R Y

LONDON • NEW DELHI • NEW YORK • SYDNEY

Bloomsbury Methuen Drama

An imprint of Bloomsbury Publishing Plc

50 Bedford Square	1385 Broadway
London	New York
WC1B 3DP	NY 10018
UK	USA

www.bloomsbury.com

Bloomsbury is a registered trade mark of Bloomsbury Publishing Plc

First published by Bloomsbury Methuen Drama 2012

Visit www.bloomsbury.com to find out more about our authors and their books
You will find extracts, author interviews, author events and you can sign up for
newsletters to be the first to hear about our latest releases and special offers.

British Library Cataloguing-in-Publication Data
A catalogue record for this book is available from the British Library.

ISBN: PB: 978-1-4081-7255-1
ePDF: 978-1-4081-7257-5
ePUB: 978-1-4081-7256-8

Library of Congress Cataloging-in-Publication Data
A catalog record for this book is available from the Library of Congress.

Snookered

Characters

Billy
Shaf
Kamy
Mo
Dave

Scene One

We are in a nook of a snooker hall; there is a pool table, some chairs and a small table. In the background we can hear the occasional arrival or departure of snooker players and people ordering drinks, but generally it has the hushed tones of a snooker hall. At the pool table is **Shaf**. *He is hitting the cue ball up and down the pool table, wasting time. After a moment he takes a mobile phone out of his pocket and switches it on. He looks at the time, turns it off and returns it to his pocket. He goes to the drinks table, drains a pint, retrieves a holdall from under it and leaves.* **Billy** *enters. He looks around, looks at his watch and notices the cue on the table, goes over and picks it up.* **Shaf** *returns.* **Billy** *has his back turned.*

Shaf Wats dat den you fackin norvern monkey . . .

Billy *turns.*

Billy Where have you been you fat bastard?

The two friends hug; there is a lot of love between them. **Shaf** *holds on a moment too long. When they part* **Billy** *gives* **Shaf** *a look.* **Shaf** *puts his bag back under the table.*

Billy I've been trying to phone you all day.

Shaf Soz bro, I forgot to put it on charge . . . what you drinking?

Billy I'll have a Bud.

Shaf A Bud! A fucking Bud! You need to move back up here bro; you'll end up smoking Marlboro lights and sucking cock.

Billy You already suck cock . . . you suck cock for Pakistan . . . you're a cocksucking international . . .

Shaf . . . with a record number of caps . . .

The two are laughing heartily by the time they reach the bar. **Dave** *the barman gets ready to serve them.*

Shaf A pint of lager, a bottle of Bud for Sheila . . . do you want a shot?

Billy   I'm alright.

Shaf   Two shots of JD please . . . is there a pay phone in here mate?

Dave   No.

Billy   Here use mine.

Shaf   No it's alright . . . it wasn't important.

Dave *starts to get the drinks together.*

Shaf   Whor phir fuckna . . . you're a dodgy cunt you.

Billy   What?

Shaf   No calls, no texts . . . no fuck all.

Billy   It's been mad bro.

Dave *puts the drinks on the bar,* **Shaf** *pays for them and gets his change.* **Shaf** *nods towards the table and the boys carry their drinks over and sit down. They pick up the shots.*

Billy   To T.

They touch glasses but **Shaf** *doesn't say anything, they neck the shots and wash them down with beer, they sit down.* **Dave** *picks up a paper and starts to read.*

Billy   So what have I missed?

Shaf   Fuck all mate . . . Arif Tootie got twelve years.

Billy   Who the fuck is Arif Tootie?

Shaf   You know Arif Tootie . . . his sister was in our year, Shanaz, massive tits.

Billy   That little fucker with the hearing aid.

Shaf   That little fucker was selling three chabbies a week bro, imagine how much money he was clearing on three kilos of heroin a week. The silly cunt was driving around in a car worth more than his house. Coppers kicked his front door in and found seventy grand under his bed. Twenty-year-old kid, doesn't know how to wipe his own arse and he's got seventy grand under his bed . . . in the wrong business me bro.

Billy   Fucking hell.

Shaf   And get on this one bro, the mum reckons he's innocent, somebody asked her about the money and the cars and she said he had a top job . . . a top fucking job! For fuck's sake aunty, the stupid twat didn't know how to write his own name.

Billy   Poor woman.

Shaf   You're so fucking naive sometimes . . . do you think that wily old cow didn't know that her boy was up to something dodgy? When Shanaz got married they hired eight limos and you want to see the kottee they built back home, like a fucking palace.

Billy   You didn't tell me all that . . . Shanaz got married eh . . . she had wicked tits . . . even in third year.

Shaf   She had a thing for T . . . I caught him in the library with his hand up her top.

Billy   You didn't tell me that.

Shaf   He used to call her Syria.

Billy   Syria?

Shaf   You know . . . bigger tits than Jordan . . . anyway he made me promise not to say 'owt.

Billy (*chuckles*)   That was T, he could get the women . . . the amount of birds that fancied him was unbelievable . . . and everything was a secret.

Shaf (*serious*)   Wasn't it just.

Billy *throws* **Shaf** *a look. The two drink in silence a moment.*

Shaf   What time did you get into town?

Billy About ten, I had some shit to sort and I went to the kavarstan.

Shaf *looks a bit sheepish at the mention of the cemetery.*

Shaf I don't really get much chance to go to the cemetery.

There is a moment's awkward silence.

Billy How's your mum, family, everybody alright?

Shaf Yeah spot on mate, she's going to Hajj with my sister and her husband.

Billy Wicked . . . how're the kids?

Shaf Spot on bro . . . Our lass is up the stick again.

Billy Fucking hell how many is that, four?

Shaf Five.

Billy So is this one going to be number six?

Shaf No this one is going to be number five.

Billy Well . . . congratulations bro.

Shaf The silly cow won't go on the pill . . . reckons it's un-Islamic, fucking dopey twat.

Billy Get the snip.

Shaf Fuck off!

Billy (*laughing*) Why not?

Shaf I'm not getting the fucking snip . . . you get the snip.

Billy I don't get women pregnant just by looking at them.

Shaf I don't . . . it's just that . . . I've got a high sex drive.

Billy *starts laughing.*

Shaf What you laughing at . . . I got a semi on when I seen you.

Billy   I have that effect on gay people . . . It's all good bro, big families are old school.

Shaf   My family credit goes up as well.

Billy   Bonus . . . I wonder where Kamy is.

Shaf   I haven't spoke to him.

Billy   I called him yesterday . . . he said he'd be here by now . . . Mo said he'd be a bit late.

Shaf   That doesn't surprise me the fucking wanker.

Billy   Behave man; he just has to work late.

Shaf   'Course he does . . . Another shot.

Billy   I'll get 'em.

Shaf   It's alright I'll get 'em.

Billy   No my shout . . . JD.

Shaf   Yeah go on then . . . I want to talk to you about something before the others get here as well . . . I've got a proposition for you.

Billy   What?

Shaf   Get the drinks in and we'll have a craic.

Billy *heads to the bar. He looks over his shoulder at* **Shaf**, *who is draining his pint.* **Dave** *puts down the paper.*

Billy   A shot of JD mate . . . you might as well get me a pint and a bottle of Bud.

Dave   Just the one shot?

Billy (*looks at* **Shaf** *again*)   Yeah just the one.

Billy *is stood at the bar when* **Kamy** *enters. He is carrying an aluminium snooker cue case and a carrier bag. He comes to the bar and taps* **Billy** *on the shoulder and then moves to the other sides making* **Billy** *look around. He sees* **Kamy** *and the two friends hug, but not with the same intensity as before with* **Shaf**.

Kamy   How you doing mate?

Billy   I'm good man.

Kamy   What time did you get into town?

Billy   This morning, sorted some stuff out and went over to the kavarstan.

Kamy   Yeah I was there on Sunday.

There's a pause.

Billy   What you having?

Kamy   What's he on?

Billy   Pints and JDs.

Kamy   Fuck it I'll have the same.

Billy (*to* **Dave**)   Another pint and shot please mate . . . make it two shots . . . so how are you?

Kamy   Wicked mate, wicked.

Billy   How's business?

Kamy   Chock-a-block bro . . . Dad's semi-retired now, so me and our kid are running things . . . made it a bit more professional, know what I mean.

Billy (*not knowing what he means*)   Yeah.

Kamy   You'll have to nip in before you go back.

Billy   I will.

The drinks are ready. **Billy** *pays for them, gets his change and they head towards the table. We see* **Shaf** *messing about with his phone. He quickly puts it in his pocket when the lads approach.*

Kamy   Shaf you fat fuck I've been trying to phone you all day.

Shaf   I forgot to put it on charge.

He puts the drinks on the table, **Shaf** *and* **Kamy** *hug.*

Kamy   You know why that is . . . it's because you're a stupid bastard.

Shaf   Fuck off dickhead.

The lads pick up the shots and touch glasses.

Kamy   To fallen comrades.

They down the shots and chase with lager.

Shaf   Fucking fallen comrades! Where do you think you are Afghanistan?

Kamy   You know what I mean.

Shaf   Mad.

Kamy (*excited*)   You want to see the tip I got for the cue?

Kamy *very carefully removes the top half of the cue from the case.* **Shaf** *throws* **Billy** *a look.* **Kamy** *rotates the cue like it's a valuable antique.*

Kamy   It's a proper professional tip that . . . the type they use at the Crucible.

Billy   You got a new tip for it last year didn't you?

Kamy   Yeah.

Shaf   And how many times have you used it since last year?

Kamy   I haven't.

Shaf   So why the fuck did you get a new tip for it?

Kamy   Because today is T's birthday and he's not here himself so I could buy him a drink . . . I've decided that every year I'm going to buy a new tip for the cue he left me.

Shaf   Fucking hell.

Kamy   It's Stephen Hendry's cue this, T nicked it out of his car, he told me before he gave it to me . . . yeah I've decided, new tip every year.

Billy   Nice one.

Shaf   I don't believe you . . . what if he'd have given you a ping pong bat?

Kamy   He never though did he, he gave me a snooker cue . . . (*vindictively*) Anyway have you told Billy about your fight?

Billy (*annoyed*)   Have you been fighting again?

Shaf (*embarrassed*)   It's fuck all.

Kamy   Hasn't he told you Billy, it's mental . . . tell him.

Shaf   It's your fucking fault I was fighting in the first place.

Kamy   How's it my fault, I wasn't even in there.

Shaf   Exactly, if you'd have turned up I wouldn't have been in there.

Billy   What fight, in where?

Shaf   I phoned this dickhead up to come and watch the match and he fucked me off.

Kamy   I was working bro.

Billy   Which match?

Shaf   The last England game.

Kamy   They're fucking shite anyway.

Billy   Where was this?

Shaf   The Monk.

Billy   Didn't T shag the barmaid out of there?

Shaf   Yeah and she used to give you loads of free drinks 'cause she thought you'd bring T in with you . . . so I thought she might still work there, have a cheap night out.

Billy   He's been . . . it's been six years.

Shaf   She wouldn't know . . . she wasn't in there anyway.

Billy   Go on.

Shaf   So anyway I'm watching the game and having a craic with these two ghoray, and at half time one of them says to me . . . he says, 'The problem with you Asians is that you don't integrate.'

Kamy   He meant Pakis.

Shaf   Fucking right he meant Pakis.

Billy   He said Asians didn't he?

Shaf   You know fuck all, when your average white man says Asian he means . . . Paki. (*To* **Kamy**.) He thought Arif Tootie's mum didn't know he was drug dealing.

Kamy   Every fucker knew, he got twelve years him. Bill found two hundred and fifty grand under his bed.

Billy   I heard it was seventy.

Kamy   No it was definitely two hundred and fifty . . . their Shanaz had a mental pair of tits.

Billy   Didn't she just . . . Shaf told me T used to grope them in the library.

Kamy   You never told me that you fat bastard.

Billy   (*using the hand gesture for wanker*)   It was a secret.

Shaf   It was seventy grand and I'm trying to tell a fucking story here!

Billy   Sorry.

Kamy   Carry on.

Shaf   So this fucker says to me, he says, 'You Pakis don't integrate' . . . and I says to him, I say, ''ere mate I'm stood in a pub, drinking a pint, watching England play football, what more do you want me to do, get a fucking Union Jack tattooed across my cock?'

The other two find this hilarious.

Billy   So what did they say to that?

Shaf   They fucking jumped me.

Billy   What there in the bar?

Shaf   No I go for a piss and I'm stood there and I hear the door open, I look over my shoulder and it's only Nick Griffin and his pal, so I know what's coming. I wait until I think he's in striking distance and I turn and bang! I drop him like a toilet seat, good fucking night Vienna, his mate only swings at me with a bottle, a fucking Bud thank you very much, but I'm bobbing and weaving and he misses and I'm like bish bosh and he's fucking down as well. So I'm stood over them, cock still out, piss all over the place and I'm giving it the big COME ON THEN! LET'S FUCKING GO! LET'S FUCKING DO IT! The barman only walks in, thinks I'm doing a George Michael and bars me out, the cunt!

Kamy   Tell him what you did . . . go on tell him . . . this is mental.

Billy   What did you do?

Shaf   I pissed on them . . . I forced all the piss I had left out and I pissed on them . . . no fucking white bastard . . .

Dave *looks up from his paper.*

Shaf   . . . calls me a Paki and gets away with it.

Dave *returns to his reading.* **Kamy** *finds this hilarious but* **Billy** *is disturbed by it.*

Billy   But they never really called you a Paki did they?

Shaf   Haven't you been listening to what I've been telling you?

Billy   What, the whole Asian thing, I thought you were taking the piss.

Shaf   Listen if your man on the ten o'clock news says Asian, he means Asian . . . but if your man at the bus stop says

Asian he means Paki, he just hasn't got the knackers to say it
to your face . . . when he's down the pub with his mates he
won't be saying 'I was stood at the bus stop with an Asian',
it'll be 'I was at the bus stop with a Paki'.

Billy   If they can't call you an Asian because it means
they're calling you a Paki, and they can't call you a Paki
because they're calling you a Paki, what are they supposed to
call you?

Kamy   They can call me mister . . . or the don . . . I like
the don.

Shaf   Why do they have to call me anything . . . they can
call me mate . . . I don't mind them calling me mate.

Kamy   Get to the bar then mate.

Shaf   It's your fucking round you tight bastard! Poody knee
yah he only comes up here for this night once a year and
you're fucking round dodging!

Kamy (*backtracking*)   I'll pay for it . . . you just go to the bar,
I've been working all day.

Shaf   I couldn't give a fuck . . . I'm not your fucking skivvy.
Go yourself and make sure you get some change for the pool
table.

Kamy *heads to the bar. As he passes* **Shaf** *he says* . . .

Kamy   You're a lazy fucker.

Shaf   Fuck you . . . (*To* **Billy**.) I fucking hate it when he does
that . . . the daft cunt.

Billy   Chill out Shaf . . . you know he's always been a tight
bastard.

Shaf   It's not that, it's all that you go to the bar . . . I'll
pay for it, like I fucking work for him, I'm his servant or
something . . . cheeky bastard, he's become a complete dick
since he's taken over the shop . . . and he still has to do what
their old fella tells him.

Billy   I'm sure he doesn't mean anything by it.

Shaf   You don't know Billy . . . it's fucking shit here now without you . . . when are you coming back bro . . . I've got some big plans for me and you.

Billy   I'm definitely not coming back if you've got plans for me.

Shaf   Seriously mate come back . . . we can sort all that bollocks with your mum and dad out . . . I'll go round and have words.

Billy   I'll talk to you about it later mate . . . it's not that simple.

Shaf   I know you're sorted down there . . . but this will be worth your while . . . you can sort shit out . . . you still work at the same place?

Billy   Yeah.

Shaf   So that shouldn't be a problem . . . just fuck 'em off.

Billy   It's not that mate . . .

Shaf   You haven't shacked back up with Sharon have you?

Billy   'course I haven't . . . I haven't seen her for years.

Shaf   Have you got a bird then?

Billy   Nowt worth writing home about.

Shaf   So you haven't.

Billy   Knobhead.

Shaf (*laughs*)   I'm just saying you're the type of lad that would fall in love if he was having a wank.

Billy   Have you heard Russell fucking Brand, when was the last time you got fixed up Mr I've got five kids.

Shaf   I have to fight them off me.

Billy   Is that right?

Shaf I've got takeaway syndrome me mate.

Billy What the fuck's that . . . have you been to the doctors for it?

Shaf Bro people who work in chip shops don't eat fish and chips . . . after the first few days they're sick of the sight of them; likewise . . .

Billy Fucking likewise!

Shaf Likewise . . . I am now sick of the sight of tush.

Kamy *returns from the bar.*

Shaf I just knock all the pussy back now mate.

Kamy Fuck off . . . you . . . stupid . . . fucking . . . twat . . . don't believe a word he's saying Bill, he's full of shit.

Billy I know he's full of shit . . . I grew up with the daft cunt.

Kamy You shagged Marie Wallace you dirty, dirty bastard.

Billy Fuck yeah I'd forgot about that errrr . . .

Shaf Listen I used to think like Gary Lineker . . . they all count . . . some are tap-ins but some are twenty-yard screamers . . .

Billy When has Gary Lineker ever scored a twenty-yard screamer!

Kamy Shaf's never scored a twenty-yard screamer either . . . all his birds have been bundled over the line.

Shaf Fuck you two . . . I'm a one-woman man now.

Kamy A tiger never changes his spots.

Shaf Leopard! It's a fucking leopard . . . how the fuck did Uncle leave you in charge of that shop . . . I'm going to phone him up and say Uncle what the fuck have you been feeding this stupid bastard . . . he's thick as shit!

Kamy   Did you kiss Marie Wallace? . . . I bet you kissed her
. . . Billy you know he kissed her.

Shaf   Kiss my black fucking arse.

Billy *is enjoying the banter. He picks up a shot and the others follow
suit.* **Kamy** *and* **Billy** *look at* **Shaf** *to make a toast. He is silent,
after a moment he says . . .*

Shaf   Health, wealth and happiness.

Kamy   You can't say that.

Shaf   I can say what I want.

Kamy   It's got to be about T.

Shaf   Why has it got to be about him?

Kamy   Because tonight is about T . . . so the . . .

Billy   The toast.

Kamy   Yeah the toast has to be about T.

Shaf   We've had a toast about him.

Billy   To health, wealth, happiness and Talub Hussein . . .
get it down your necks.

The lads down the shots and drink lager, **Kamy** *feeds the pool table
money and starts to set the balls up.* **Shaf** *looks at* **Billy** *and shakes
his head,* **Billy** *isn't sure why.*

Kamy   Who am I going to beat first then?

Shaf   You play him Billy then I'll beat him.

Billy   Fuck off I'll play the winner.

Kamy *goes to the case and very delicately starts to assemble the cue.*
Shaf *goes and takes one off a rack on the wall.*

Kamy   You break.

Shaf   Fuck off you break.

Kamy *winks at* **Billy**.

Kamy   Losers break.

Shaf   We haven't played a game yet.

Kamy   Last time we played you lost, so you break.

Shaf   Just fucking break.

Billy   For fuck's sake.

Kamy   We'll toss for it.

Shaf   Heads.

Kamy *picks a coin up from the side of the table and flips; he catches it, has a look himself and then shows* **Shaf***.*

Shaf   Wanker.

Shaf *breaks, the lads start playing; the conversation takes place in between shots.*

Kamy   This is my lucky cue . . . every time I play with it I do really well, I'm sure T is looking down on me helping pot the balls.

Shaf   How many other cues have you got?

Kamy   Just this one.

Shaf   So it's not your lucky cue; it's your only cue dickhead.

Kamy   It can still be my lucky cue . . . can't it Bill?

Billy   It can mate.

Shaf   How can it?

Billy   Because he feels lucky when he's using it.

Shaf   But that doesn't make it lucky . . . it'd be lucky if when he was using a different cue he was shit . . . but then when he picked this one up he was like Ronnie O'Sullivan . . . then . . . then he could say this is my lucky cue . . . otherwise it's just another fucking cue.

Kamy   But it's not just another cue, it's the cue T gave me.

Shaf   What's that got to do with the price of lamb chops!
Shall I tell you something about that fucking cue . . .

We see **Billy** *shaking his head vigorously behind* **Kamy**. **Shaf** *spots this and hesitates a moment.*

Shaf   . . . For fuck's sake . . . alright it's your lucky fucking
cue . . . can we carry on with the game now?

They restart the game; **Kamy** *takes a shot while* **Shaf** *drains his pint.*

Billy   You need to slow down Shaf.

Shaf   We're on a night out aren't we . . . drink up.

Billy   I'm alright.

Shaf   You're not in London now with your homosexual
friends.

Kamy *drains his drink as well.*

Kamy   Come on Billy get it down.

Billy *reluctantly drains his bottle,* **Shaf** *heads to the bar.*

Billy   Can't you lot take your time, it's not a fucking race.

Kamy   It's a night out bro . . . make the most of it, that's
what I say.

Billy   So what's been happening?

Kamy   Fuck all.

Billy   There must have been something going on.

Kamy *thinks a moment.*

Kamy   . . . Remember Sajjy Iqbal, he got shot.

Billy   Who'd want to shoot him, he was fucking harmless
. . . is he dead?

Kamy   No it was in the leg . . . Like fucking Helmand
Province here mate . . . these young kids bro . . . they're

making that much money off the drugs . . . anybody fucks with them . . . they'll be at your front door next day . . . a van load of them . . . don't care if your mum or your sister's there . . . just do you over . . . baseball bats, guns.

Billy   Don't tell me Sajjy Iqbal was mixed up with that?

Kamy   No mate . . . This was over a parking space.

Billy   Fuck off.

Kamy   I'm telling you Bill . . . over a parking space . . . argued with this Ditta character one night, big-time drug dealer . . . real nasty fucker Bill . . . the next day a lad in a balaclava shot him in the leg.

Billy   Didn't they arrest him?

Kamy   He got away.

Billy   What about this Ditta?

Kamy   Had an alibi . . . he was sat in the magistrates court, had him on CCTV walking in and then leaving two hours later . . . they reckon he's behind any amounts of shootings and shit like that . . .

Billy   Fucking mad that . . . what's happening with the lads?

Kamy   To tell you the truth Bill, I'm that busy with the shop I hardly see anybody.

Billy   Business booming then.

Kamy   It's bouncing mate . . . me and our kid have got big plans . . . go up market . . . change the name and everything . . . what do you reckon to A to Z?

Billy   Sorry?

Kamy   Ya know, new name for the shop, A to Z butchers.

Billy   Do butchers go from A to Z?

Kamy   Ours will.

Billy   How?

Kamy   Complete service from A to Z . . . we cover
everything.

Billy   Right . . . what do you call it now?

Kamy   Kharee Halal Meats . . . from where the old fella's
from back home.

Billy   I don't know mate . . . when you say A to Z, a
butchers isn't the first thing that comes to mind.

Kamy   Is it not . . . what do you think we should call it?

Billy   Why do you want to change it anyway? . . . it's
established, people know it.

Kamy   We want to go up market bro . . . supply schools,
hospitals . . . corporate shit . . . they have to feed every
fucker halal meat now. Kharee Halal Meats makes us sound
like . . . I don't know . . . it makes us sound like refugees or
something.

Billy *thinks a moment.*

Billy   How about KHM . . . KHM supplies . . . KHM Foods.

Kamy   KHM Foods . . . KHM Foods . . . I like the sound of
that . . . KHM Foods.

Shaf *returns from the bar.*

Kamy   What do you reckon to KHM Foods?

Shaf   What?

Kamy   For the shop . . . new name KHM Foods.

Shaf *thinks a moment.*

Shaf   You're called Kamran, your kid's called Khadam . . .
why don't you call it KKC?

Kamy   KKC?

Shaf   KKC.

Shaf *picks up his shot, the others follow. We can see that* **Kamy** *is still trying to work out what KKC means.*

Billy   T.

The lads touch glasses and drink. A light bulb comes on in **Kamy**'s *head.*

Kamy (*eureka!*)   Kamran Khadam Catering.

Shaf   No . . . Kamran Khadam Cunts.

Billy *and* **Shaf** *start laughing,* **Kamy** *is not amused.*

Kamy   Yes very funny . . . I think if you leave the thinking to those of us who can . . . and when we need some dickhead to run us around in a taxi we can call you.

Now it's **Shaf**'s *turn to be stung by* **Kamy**'s *remarks.*

Shaf   What thinking can you do on your own, you cabbage?

Kamy   More than you . . . that cue ball's got more brains than you.

Billy   Can we finish the game please?

Shaf   You were in bottom set Kamy you retard.

Billy   You were both as thick as shit . . . me and T were in top set . . . so can we finish the game please.

Shaf *and* **Kamy** *look at each other, it's like that then is it?*

Shaf   You were only in top set because you let Mr Ball feel your arse.

Kamy   Yeah you used to go to his classroom at dinner time and give him a nosh.

Billy *is not fazed by the other two ganging up on him.*

Billy   Dumb and fucking Dumber. I was in top set because I passed exams . . . if you two wanted to be in top set you'd have to give the whole staff room a nosh . . . by the way how many exams did you two pass?

Shaf   I would have done alright me . . . but I got suspended for smacking Stuart Asperly . . . that fucking Whitaker seen me from the science labs . . . he was a fucking racist.

Kamy   You and T made me nick off when the exams were on . . . you pair of bastards.

Shaf   Like you would have set the world on fire if you sat your exams.

Kamy   You never know . . . why didn't T sit his exams? . . . he'd have done alright . . . you know one year when we were in Mrs Batty's class together he did my homework for me for a full year.

Shaf   Didn't she clock on?

Kamy   No . . . he used to tell me what to write . . . show me how to do it . . . he was a clever cunt.

Shaf   He can't have been that clever or he'd have sat his exams . . . got some qualifications . . . I tell you what though . . . if I was back at school now, I'd be a proper swot . . . get my head down do all my work . . . no fucking about.

Kamy   Yeah as if that would make a difference.

Shaf   Of course it would . . .

Billy   Oh for fuck's sake . . . trust me it isn't Mr Whitaker's fault that you two aren't fucking nuclear scientists.

This gets a chuckle.

Shaf   Yeah but I might not have been a taxi driver . . . I still see that cunt when I pick my Sophie up.

Billy   Sophie goes to Cunningham . . . I'd love to go back see what it's like.

Shaf   Spot the white kid in there mate.

Kamy   Nowt wrong with that.

Billy   I don't know like.

Shaf Did you hear about that eleven-year-old white girl wanted to convert to Islam, she was at Cunningham?

Kamy Nowt wrong with that either.

Shaf You know what happened there . . . her best mate was probably an apnee, the girl comes round to play and the mum says that anybody who isn't a Muslim is going straight to hell, poor girl's probably shitting herself, thinks that if you don't wear a hijab you're getting shit GCSE results.

Billy It's bad news that.

Kamy Why?

Billy Because if you're a Paki at home . . . you don't need to be a Paki at school as well.

Kamy If you don't keep the kids on the right path you're just going to end up with a load of coconuts . . . no offence Billy.

Billy What do you mean no offence Billy, I'm not a coconut.

Kamy You are mate. (*To* **Shaf**.) He is, isn't he?

Shaf You are a bit like Billy.

Billy I'm not a fucking coconut . . . you two think that because I don't think that all white people are bastards there's something wrong with me.

Shaf I'm not saying they're all bastards . . . I'm just saying that they're not like us.

Kamy Ghoray don't give a fuck.

Billy What's that supposed to mean, ghoray don't give a fuck?

Shaf I've had white lads in my taxi who'll say to their mate, shit like 'Tell your sister I'd lick her pussy.' What type of bullshit is that . . . I mean fucking hell bro if that's not different from us I don't know what is.

Billy   But that's different, that's . . .

Shaf   When you were with Sharon and her brother seen you two . . .

Billy   She hasn't got a brother.

Shaf   Well her cousin then dickhead . . . he might say (*in a camp voice*) 'Now then Shazza, now then Bill, do you fancy a pint, do you fancy a cuppa . . .?'

Billy   Gay cousin is it?

Shaf   Yeah probably . . . but say if you were banging the arse off an apnee girl and one of her relatives seen you together he'd want to cut your heart out with a rusty fucking knife.

Billy   But that's all changing now.

Shaf   But the brother still wants to kill you even after you've married her and had fifteen fucking kids.

Billy   That doesn't mean that you can say all Pakis are like this or all ghoray are like that.

Kamy   Yes you can.

Shaf   Some things are white.

Billy   But they're not exclusively white.

Shaf   Some are.

Billy   Like what?

The lads start to think of an exclusively white trait.

Kamy   White people let dogs lick their faces.

Billy   What about khutaa Rasheed . . . That fucker used to feed his kids dhal and feed his rottweilers gosht . . . so it's not that.

Shaf   Yeah Rash, he was dirty bastard . . . white people eat pig.

Billy *immediately looks at* **Kamy** *who is not happy with the turn the conversation has taken.*

Billy   Is that right Kamy, do only white people sneak out of the cinema to have a hotdog with mustard and onions?

Kamy *is looking very sheepish.*

Kamy   I'm sure there's some apney who eat pork.

Shaf   Poody knee yah you run a fucking halal butchers!

Kamy   What!

Shaf   Eating fucking hotdogs you dodgy bastard.

Kamy   Who ate hotdogs? I didn't eat hotdogs.

Shaf   I can tell by that look on your face, you're a lying bastard.

Kamy   I didn't eat no fucking hotdogs, T was the one who used to eat hotdogs . . . anyway you can get halal sausages as well nowadays.

Shaf   Not in fucking Cineworld!

Billy   You can now . . .

Shaf   It's difficult to put my finger on it right now, but there are things that are different.

Billy   But they're not exclusive to one or the other, that's what I'm saying.

Kamy   You don't see apney in old people's homes.

Billy   What?

Kamy   You only see white people in old people's homes.

Shaf   There you go, we look after our own, we don't just dump them in homes.

Billy   You see them in homes down south.

Shaf   That's because they're a bunch of cockney wankers. How can you just abandon your parents?

*It's **Billy**'s turn to look a bit sheepish. **Shaf** realises what he has said.*

Shaf   I didn't mean you . . . yours is a different situation.

Billy   I know you never mate.

Shaf   Sorry mate . . . I didn't mean you.

Billy   Don't worry about it.

Shaf   I feel like a dick mate.

Kamy   That's because you are a dick.

Shaf   Shut up, daft cunt.

Billy   Look let's just forget about it . . . whose shot is it?

The lads go back to playing pool.

Kamy   Shaf where's your fucking cousin?

Shaf   He's not my cousin alright . . . knobhead's probably in the mosque.

Billy (*surprised*)   How long's he been going to the mosque?

Kamy   He's seen the light . . . I'm going to start going.

Shaf   Dickhead . . . you only want to go to the mosque when you're pissed.

Billy   He never mentioned anything to me.

Shaf   Have you been talking to him?

Billy   Just a couple of times . . . is he hardcore?

Kamy   I wouldn't say he was hardcore . . . but he's got plenty of books and stuff . . . he hasn't declared war on America if that's what you're thinking.

Shaf   So did you phone him or did he phone you?

Billy   What? I don't remember . . . it was just a couple times.

Shaf   Didn't phone me though.

Billy   Who never?

Shaf   You never.

Kamy   Oh for fuck's sake.

Shaf   I'm just saying.

Billy   I've spoke to him a couple of times . . . does it matter?

Kamy (*winding* **Shaf** *up*)   So who put the phone down first Bill, you or him?

Billy (*joining in*)   Well I was saying to him 'you first' and he was saying 'no, you first' and the next thing you know the sun had come up.

Kamy   That's dead romantic . . . has he asked you to marry him yet?

Billy   I think tonight's the night.

Shaf   You're a pair of fucking knobheads.

Billy *and* **Kamy** *start laughing.*

Shaf   I tell you what though; if he starts any of his jihad bullshit tonight I'm wrapping this fucking cue around his head.

Billy   Leave him be man . . . it's a good thing.

Shaf   It's all bollocks, I don't even believe in it.

Kamy   Don't believe in what?

Shaf   All that religion shit.

Kamy   You're going to burn in hell.

Billy   How long have you thought like that?

Shaf Bro a couple of hundred years ago everybody thought the Earth was flat, in a few more years, everybody will know that there's no such thing as God.

Kamy (*upset*) Tauba Tauba . . . bastra you can't say things like that!

Shaf You eat fucking pork! What type of Muslim are you?

Kamy So fuck! I still believe in God!

Shaf That's because you're a fucking idiot.

Kamy Fuck you!

Billy Have you told your mum?

Shaf Of course not . . . she'd have a fucking heart attack.

Billy You surprised me there like mate . . . but if that's what you think, that's what you think.

Kamy Don't be saying things like that to him Bill . . . you're just encouraging the daft bastard . . . this is all down to the Discovery Channel this.

Shaf What are you going on about?

Billy What's the Discovery Channel got to do with it?

Kamy The daft bastard watches the Discovery Channel all night and it's putting ideas into his head. What the dickhead doesn't realise is that that's just propaganda spread by the white man to make you believe that it's alright not to believe in God, and he's fucking fallen for it.

*The lads find this very funny but **Kamy** is genuinely upset.*

Kamy Don't fucking laugh! It's not fucking funny!

Billy It is mate.

Kamy Shall I tell you what . . . that's some bad shit he's talking there. We're fucking Muslims – we're under attack as it is without daft cunts like him talking bullshit!

Shaf   What the fuck's got into you?

Kamy   You and your bullshit, you think you're a clever cunt but you're not, don't be talking your bollocks where I am.

Shaf   Ooooooo.

Kamy   Fuck you!

Kamy *storms off to the toilets,* **Billy** *raises his eyebrows.*

Billy   That was a bit mad.

Shaf   Fuck him, he's a drama queen.

Billy   Were you just winding him up?

Shaf   No . . . it's all man-made bollocks . . . I'm surprised at you . . . I'd have thought you were like me.

Billy   Why?

Shaf *thinks a moment.*

Shaf   I don't know I just did . . . but you don't pray or anything.

Billy   I know but I still believe in God . . . I'm still a Muslim.

Shaf   Why? There's no proof he exists.

Billy   That's why it's called faith.

Shaf (*nodding towards the drink*)   He's going to be pissed off with you then.

Billy   Not as much as he going to be pissed of with you.

They both chuckle and then fall silent a moment.

Shaf   I didn't mean anything earlier with all that abandoning your parents shit.

Billy   I know you never, forget about it.

Shaf   You need to come back though . . . you and Sharon that was years ago . . . if you want I'll get my mum to go round and have words . . . your mum and dad will be alright.

Billy I'll have a craic with you later . . . (*Changing the subject.*) it must be mad around yours then with Mo doing the whole religion thing.

Shaf Everybody thinks the sun shines out of his fucking arse . . . my sandhu is a gandhu.

Billy What's a sandhu?

Shaf You're a fucking coconut you . . . don't you know what a sandhu is . . . it's your wife's sister's husband.

Billy You mean your brother-in-law.

Shaf Yeah but wife's brother is your brother-in-law as well, but your sandhu is your wife's sister's husband . . . and mine's a fucking prick.

Billy He's alright Mo . . . you two were tight.

Shaf You know fuck all mate . . . he's a fucking snake . . . and he thinks he's something special because he wears a suit to work.

Billy You can't be pissed with him because he wears a suit to work, that's his job.

Shaf It's not just the suit mate, it's because . . . it's his know-it-all attitude . . . because everybody is like 'ask Mo . . . Mo will know what to do' . . . it's gone to his head. I mean for fuck's sake he's Assistant Manger at a Comet store, he's not Stephen fucking Fry.

Billy (*laughing*) It's not his fault that they all want his opinion.

Shaf I wouldn't mind mate, but it's how he goes about it. He sits there in the recliner with his chin in his hand . . . deep in thought like he's solving global fucking warming and all they've asked him is whether British Gas is better than Scottish Power.

Billy You're mad you.

They're both laughing.

Shaf It's true mate . . . and nobody can see he's full of shit
. . . it's all Mo this, Mo that, Mo's gone to the gym . . . Mo's
gone to read jumma . . . Mo's firing blanks . . . (**Billy** *stops
laughing.*) Mo can't get his wife pregnant . . . the fucking
prick.

Billy That's a bit strong mate.

Shaf Fuck him it's true . . . anyway I've got enough
problems of my own to be worried about him.

Billy What's up?

Shaf Bro, I might have got myself into a little jam.

Billy What have you done now?

Shaf (*angry*) Fucking hell! . . .

We see **Kamy** *returning from the toilet.* **Shaf** *spots him.*

Shaf . . . I'll tell you later.

Billy (*to* **Kamy**) Alright.

Kamy Sorted . . . whose round is it?

Shaf Yours.

Billy It's mine, what we having? . . . same again?

The lads nod and **Billy** *heads towards the bar. There is a moment's
awkward silence between* **Shaf** *and* **Kamy**.

Shaf What's got into you?

Kamy Just forget about it.

Shaf Please yourself.

Kamy You're a fucking knob.

Shaf If you want me to lie to you I will . . . I believe in God
. . . there, are you happy? . . . What time is it?

Kamy *shows him his watch,* **Shaf** *looks at the watch and reaches into his pocket. He pauses a moment remembering something, looks at* **Kamy***, who is still sulking a bit, then comes to a decision.*

Shaf   Lend us your phone.

Kamy *hands him the phone,* **Shaf** *takes his own phone out of his pocket, turns it on, finds a number and dials on* **Kamy***'s phone. As he is waiting for someone to pick up, he turns his own phone off and returns it to his pocket. The call isn't answered and* **Shaf** *returns the phone.*

Kamy   I thought you said your phone was dead?

Shaf   I said it's fucked.

Kamy   What's up with it?

Shaf   I can't get a signal on it.

Kamy   Show us . . . you just need to do a network search . . . it's happened to mine.

Shaf   It's alright I'll sort it later.

Kamy   Just show it here . . . it only takes a minute.

Shaf   I've said I'll sort it later.

Kamy   Why don't you sort it now? . . . I know what to do.

Shaf   When I need a goat chopping up I'll come see you . . . when I need my phone fixing I'll go and see a . . . a phone fixer.

Kamy   What the fuck is a phone fixer?

Shaf   Somebody who's not a fucking butcher.

Billy *returns with the drinks, the lads pick up the shots.*

Kamy   Talub.

Billy   Talub.

Shaf *again remains silent and the boys neck their drinks.*

Lights fade.

Scene Two

Billy *and* **Shaf** *are playing pool, the bottles and glasses have built up on the table,* **Kamy** *is sat admiring his cue. He looks at his watch and then looks at* **Shaf***.*

Kamy   What time's your cousin getting here? . . . I want to start the game.

Shaf   He's not my fucking cousin . . . and we're already playing a game.

Kamy   You know what I mean . . . the doubles.

Shaf   Do we have to play pool all night? . . . It's the same year in year out.

Kamy   We always play pool . . . it's tradition.

Shaf   It's fucking boring.

Kamy   You only think it's boring because you're shit.

Shaf   It's because I can't be arsed . . . if I wanted to I'd kick your arse.

Kamy   Yeah right . . . you couldn't beat me if your life depended on it.

Shaf   I tell you what . . . if I win tonight . . . I want that cue.

Billy   Behave Shaf.

Kamy   No chance.

Shaf   What's the matter . . . your arse gone?

Billy   Shaf man . . . leave it.

Shaf   The dickhead's always going on about how good he is . . . well if he's that good . . . It won't be a problem.

Kamy   What do I get if I win?

Shaf   Fuck all . . . I aren't the one who's shooting his mouth off.

Kamy   Well that's not a bet then is it?

Shaf   What do you want?

Thinks a moment.

Kamy   If I win . . . I want . . . let me think about it.

Shaf   Fucking knew it . . . full of shit.

Billy   How can you bet anyway? . . . we play doubles.

Kamy   No I'll think of something . . . the problem is Bill the daft cunt's got fuck all that I want.

Shaf   What the fuck's that supposed to mean you prick?

Billy   Behave the pair of you.

Shaf   No, I want to know what he means by that.

Kamy   This cue is that valuable that I'd have to bet you for your house.

Billy   Kamy leave it bro.

Shaf   You fucking daft cunt, that fucking cue . . .

The doors open and **Mo** *enters. The lads stop talking.*

Billy   I thought you weren't going to turn up.

Mo   Can't miss tonight.

Mo *comes over to the lads and gives* **Billy** *a big hug. He then hugs* **Kamy**, *he only shakes* **Shaf**'s *hand, he says to* **Shaf**:

Mo   What's up with your phone? . . . they're trying to get in touch with you at home.

Shaf   I'll phone them in a bit.

Mo (*to* **Billy**)   Sorry mate . . . we've got a promotion starting on tellies in the morning . . . they needed me to sort it out.

Billy   Don't worry about it.

Shaf   Must be a nightmare putting those sale stickers up without supervision.

Mo *ignores him.*

Billy How you doing mate?

Mo Allah na Shukar bro.

Kamy *and* **Shaf** *look at each other and roll their eyes.*

Mo What time did you get into town?

Billy About ten.

Mo Everything alright?

Billy Yeah.

Mo Does anybody want a drink?

Billy We're alright.

Shaf Two pints, a bottle of Bud and three shots of JD.

Mo Anything else?

Kamy That's it.

Mo *heads to the bar.*

Billy I thought you said he was all Osama Bin Laden?

Shaf Didn't you hear all that Allah na Shukar patter?

Billy You're off it you . . . he's getting the drinks in isn't he?

Shaf I bet you he gets himself an orange juice or something.

Kamy He'll be lecturing us about drinking before the night's out.

Shaf It won't even take him that long.

Kamy I think he'll wait till we're having something to eat.

Shaf He'll do it whilst we're still in here.

Billy You're mad you two.

Shaf   I'm telling you, I give it half an hour.

Kamy   You're wrong . . . longer.

Shaf   I bet you.

Kamy   A pound.

Billy   Behave lads.

Shaf   A fucking pound! Twenty quid.

Billy   Don't be daft.

Kamy   No . . . just a pound.

Shaf   Tight bastard . . . alright then a pound . . . what time is it?

Billy (*looks at his watch*)   Half eight.

Shaf   Kamy lend me your phone.

Kamy *looks at him, shakes his head and hands his phone over.* **Shaf** *presses the dial key twice and puts the phone to his ear . . . no answer. He hands the phone back to* **Kamy**. *Mo returns from the bar with the drinks that the lads ordered and a coke for himself.* **Shaf** *and* **Kamy** *look at* **Billy** *– we told you so. The lads pick up the shots and* **Mo** *gets his coke, they touch glasses.*

Kamy   To absent friends.

Billy *and* **Mo** *together . . .*

Billy   Absent friends.

Mo   Absent friends.

Shaf *doesn't say anything, but instead watches* **Mo** *sip his drink with a look of contempt on his face.*

Shaf   That hit the spot . . . can't beat a good shot of JD . . . I fancy getting off my face tonight.

Kamy *looks at* **Shaf**.

Kamy   Mo you work in Comet, what do they call people who fix mobile phones?

Shaf *turns to stare at* **Kamy**.

Shaf   Fucking dickhead.

Mo   Phone engineer.

Billy   I thought they were the gadgies that had the green boxes open at the end of your street.

Mo   Telecoms engineers then.

Kamy   I think you're right.

Shaf   That Ifty who's got the phone shop, he fixes phones and believe me he's no engineer.

Mo   The phone shops usually just unblock them or change screens . . . simple stuff . . . anything more complicated and they have to send them away.

Kamy   Is that what they do in your shop?

Mo   We don't do any repairs in-house.

A moment's silence.

Shaf   The point is they don't use a fucking butcher.

Billy   What are you two going on about?

Shaf   Nowt.

Kamy   He won't let me fix his phone.

Mo   What's up with your phone?

Kamy   He can't get a signal.

Billy   Do a network search.

Shaf   What are we all fucking phone experts now? . . . I've said I'll sort it . . . and I don't need this useless cunt to do it for me.

Mo   They want you to phone home.

Shaf   Yeah you've fucking said! . . . can we play some fucking pool?

Kamy   Finish your game and we'll get the doubles started.

Mo   Give us a minute, let me chill a bit.

Kamy *looks disappointed,* **Billy** *and* **Shaf** *go back to the pool game.*

Kamy   Mo I needed some advice.

Shaf *looks at* **Billy** *and rolls his eyes,* **Billy** *suppresses a laugh.*

Mo   What about mate?

Kamy   Say if I wanted to supply a school with halal meat how would I go about it?

Shaf   He works for Comet . . . what the fuck are you asking him for?

Mo   I'm the Assistant Manager . . . I would suggest that you contact the relevant school and arrange a meeting with the headmaster . . . or alternatively contact the LEA.

Shaf (*to* **Kamy**)   Have you made a note of that in your filofax . . . you daft cunt.

Billy   Shaf.

Shaf   Explain it to him in a language he understands.

Kamy   If you're that clever how come you're still driving a taxi?

Shaf   I might drive a taxi, but I wouldn't ask stupid questions like that . . . it's fucking obvious what you've got to do.

Kamy   Alright then . . . what about hospitals?

Not sure of himself now.

Shaf   Well . . . you do the same thing.

Kamy   What? . . . Go to the LEA? . . . You fucking knobhead.

Mo   I think he meant that you should contact . . .

Shaf   I know what I meant . . . this dickhead doesn't though
. . . contact whoever's supplying the food and do a deal with
them.

Billy   I think they buy the cooked food in Kamy.

Kamy   But how do I find out who supplies the food?

Shaf   Shall I tell you what? Stick to selling half a pound of
lamb leg to old women, because you haven't got a fucking
clue.

Billy   Fucking ignore him Kamy . . . that's how you learn
about these things . . . by asking people.

Kamy   I pay no notice to him Billy . . . he knows fuck all
anyway.

Shaf   We'll see who knows what.

Billy   Sounds ominous . . . what are you up to?

Shaf   I've got a couple of irons in a couple of fires mate . . .
things are looking up.

Kamy   What you doing?

Shaf   You just stick to skinning chickens son.

Kamy   You probably want to open a car wash.

Mo   Good money in those car washes if you can get the
right location.

Shaf   It's not a fucking car wash . . . do I look like I the type
of person who washes cars?

Billy   Actually you do.

Kamy   You know what I've learnt from business? Money
makes money.

Shaf   Who the fuck are you, James Caan?

Billy   Who's James Caan?

Mo   'Dragons' Den'.

Shaf   Those dragons would be fighting each other to invest in me.

Mo   Invest in your business.

Shaf   This is where you are wrong . . . they invest in the person not the idea.

Kamy   Who the fuck's going to invest in you? . . . I'd rather put my money in the Albanian Stock Exchange.

The others laugh.

Shaf   Laugh all you want . . . but you'll be sick as fuck when I'm rolling in it.

Billy   So what's this idea then Shaf?

Shaf   Sort your shit out and get back here . . . because you're going to be my partner.

Billy   Thanks but no thanks.

Shaf   I'll talk to you about it later . . .

Mo   So what you been up to then Billy?

Billy   Same ole same ole bro.

Mo   Where about London do you live?

Billy   Forest Gate.

Mo   How far is that from Enfield?

Billy   Not far, why?

Mo   I might be getting a job there mate.

Billy   Really, that's wicked that bro.

Shaf   What job's this?

Mo   I applied for the Manager's post at the Enfield branch . . . I've got the interview in a couple of weeks.

Billy That's brilliant . . . I'll have someone to chill with.

Shaf Do they know at home?

Mo Of course they know at home.

Shaf What did they say?

Mo Nothing.

Shaf They must have said something?

Mo They're just hoping I get it.

Kamy Are you taking the missus?

Mo I've got to get the job first.

Billy Come down a couple of days early and we'll chill, I'll show you around London, you can see where I live . . . why don't all of you come down? . . . It'll be a buzz.

Mo I will.

Shaf *has started to brood. We see him taking big gulps of his drink.*

Kamy You're game as fuck Mo . . . what if you don't like it?

Mo I'll come back . . . but the plan is if I get the job, work down there for a couple of years and if a Manager's job comes up here, apply for it and maybe move back . . . But if I like it I'd stay . . . and you know this could lead to Regional Manager . . . company car, the works.

Shaf Well it's alright for you . . . no kids and that . . . you're laughing.

Billy Shaf!

Shaf What, I'm just saying . . . I'm right; it's easier if you haven't got kids.

Kamy London would be alright if it wasn't full of cockneys.

Billy They're alright man.

Kamy If you've got a black cat, they'll have a blacker one.

Shaf   It's fucking shit.

Billy   How would you know?

Shaf   I was down there for a wedding once . . . fucking shit.

Shaf *picks up his glass and finishes his drink, slams the glass on the table. A little harder than he really wanted to.*

Shaf   Right then same again.

Billy   I'm taking it easy me . . . I'm alright.

Shaf   Fuck you . . . drink for drink . . . (*To* **Mo**.) What you drinking?

Mo   I'm alright thanks.

Shaf   Have a drink.

Mo   No thanks.

Shaf   Are you driving?

Mo   No.

Shaf   Well have a drink then.

Mo   I don't want one.

Shaf   Don't worry I won't tell your lass.

Billy   He said he doesn't want one.

Shaf   Why not, what's wrong with him?

Billy   There's fuck all wrong with him . . . he just doesn't want one.

Mo   I'll have one next time.

Shaf   You don't mind if we have one do you.

Mo   Knock yourself out.

Shaf   I'm the only fucker who could . . . right then you two dickheads I want them finished when I get back.

Shaf *heads to the bar.*

Billy I hope you get it mate.

Mo I do.

Kamy Are you going to give us a hand finding out about these schools and stuff before you go?

Mo Yeah of course I will.

Kamy Tomorrow?

Mo Not tomorrow . . . give us a couple of days.

Kamy When?

Mo I don't know . . . I'll call you . . . or I'll nip in the shop.

Kamy No don't come into the shop . . . just call me.

Billy Why can't he come to the shop?

Kamy It's too mad in there . . . you can't really talk . . . loads of crazy aunties coming in and out all the time . . . I'll be glad to get this sorted so I don't have to deal with them.

Billy So you want to get away from the aunties then Kamy?

Kamy Billy kid, what a fucking nightmare . . . They come in want to haggle over everything . . . want credit . . . when I start talking in Punjabi they start taking the piss . . . or they'll want the old fella to sort it out for them.

Billy I bet they do . . . anyway I thought you said he'd retired?

Kamy That's what he said but he's there every day . . . does my head in if I'm honest.

Mo Why?

Kamy He's got a bit of a temper on him . . . and he'll start going to town on me in front of the customers . . . it's fucking embarrassing bro.

Mo He's your dad . . . what can you say?

Kamy   That's why I want to box this school thing off . . . maybe he'd chill out then . . . let me and our kid crack on with things . . . we've got big plans.

Shaf *returns from the bar. He's got tequila, and has all the paraphernalia.*

Billy   What the fuck's that?

Shaf   Tequila!

Billy   Why did you get them you loon?

Shaf   We're fucking celebrating Mo's new job aren't we?

Mo   I haven't got it yet.

Kamy   We're supposed to be celebrating T's birthday.

Shaf   Fuck him.

Shaf *laughs but the others are shocked that he's said that.*

Shaf   Cheer up you miserable fuckers . . . I was joking . . . he'd have laughed at that . . . here's something else we can celebrate . . . I'm having another baby.

Billy *gives* **Shaf** *a real hard look.*

Mo (*gives* **Shaf** *a long hard look*)   Yeah I've heard.

Kamy   What you trying to do get a football team?

Shaf   Matey my spunk's so fertile . . . I'm going to leave it to science . . . let's get these down our necks.

The lads go through the ritual and down the tequila.

Billy   That's fucking disgusting.

Shaf   Put fucking hair on your chest that fucking gear.

Kamy   I'm not having any more of them.

Shaf   Shut up you fanny.

Billy   No wonder you have to suck on a lemon.

Mo *is watching with a look of distaste on his face.*

Kamy   Right, I'm setting the balls up . . . doubles.

Shaf   More fucking pool . . . I thought we were going to chill for a bit.

Billy   Kamy if you want to set the balls up . . . go for it . . . are you sorted Mo?

Mo   Sorted.

Kamy   Me and Billy . . . against you and Mo.

Shaf   Fuck off . . . Me and Billy against you and Mo.

Billy   We'll pick numbers.

Kamy   I'll go and get some more change.

Kamy *doesn't move but instead stares at* **Shaf***. After a moment* **Shaf** *realises why* **Kamy** *hasn't left, just shakes his head and gets some pound coins out of his pocket and hands them to* **Kamy***, who takes them and heads to the bar. The lads wait a moment and then give each other numbers.* **Shaf** *is 1,* **Kamy** *is 2,* **Billy** *is 3 and* **Mo** *4.*

Mo   Has he got the T-shirts?

Billy *nods towards the carrier bag* **Kamy** *came in with. After a moment* **Kamy** *returns.*

Kamy   Have you picked?

The lads nod.

Kamy   One and Two, Three and Four.

Shaf   Fuck!

Billy   You and Shaf, me and Mo.

Kamy   Bastard!

Shaf   I wanted to torture him tonight.

Kamy   I fucking knew I'd end up with him.

Billy   Right set them up.

Mo *starts to set the balls up.*

Shaf   Can't we pick again?

Kamy   'ere I'm the best player here . . . you should be grateful I'm letting you be my partner.

Shaf   You're a fucking head buster . . . that's what you are.

Mo   Chill out lads . . . it's only a game.

Kamy   It's not just a game! This dickhead doesn't even know how to play doubles.

Billy   He's not that bad Kamy.

Shaf   What do you mean I'm not that bad? . . . It's only fucking pool . . . all you do is put the balls in the holes.

Kamy   See what I mean? . . . they're pockets not holes . . . it's not golf . . . we're partners . . . if there's nothing on, play safe . . . and leave the rest to me . . . and remember there's no i in team.

Shaf   I know but there's a u in cunt!

Mo   They're arguing already Bill . . . this'll be easy.

Kamy   We're going to kick your arse.

Billy   We'll see . . . your break.

Kamy   We'll toss for it.

Shaf   Tails.

Mo *flips a coin and shows the lads.*

Shaf   Wanker.

Kamy *just looks at* **Shaf** *and shakes his head in resignation. He breaks. The break doesn't go well.*

Shaf   What the fuck was that?

Kamy   Don't worry I'm just warming up.

Shaf   Well don't take too long.

The next set of shots is played in silence and it comes back to **Kamy**'s *shot. He lines up a shot, stands and chalks the cue, lines up the shot again, changes his mind and lines up a different shot. He aims, takes the shot and . . . misses.*

Kamy   Poody tie knee!

Shaf   You fucking useless cunt!

Mo *and* **Billy** *are laughing as . . .*

Lights fade.

Scene Three

The boys are just finishing a game as we join them. **Shaf** *and* **Kamy** *have lost.*

Shaf   What the fuck was that!

Kamy   We've pulled one back . . . anyway you aren't doing 'owt.

Mo   What we drinking?

Billy   I'll get them in . . . my shout . . . what we having?

Shaf   A pint and a shot . . . tequila.

Kamy   Just a pint for me.

Shaf   Get the fanny a shot as well.

Kamy   Those tequilas make me want to puke.

Shaf   You just need to get used to them.

Kamy   I don't want to get used to them.

Billy   What you having Mo?

Mo   I'll have a Bacardi and coke kid.

There is a moment's stunned silence.

Shaf   I thought you said you didn't drink.

Mo No, I said I don't want a drink.

Shaf You're a fucking hypocrite!

Billy Shaf!

Shaf He fucking is! Going on about being a good Muslim and all that bollocks and all the time he's drinking, he's no better than the rest of us.

Mo I didn't stop because of the religion.

Shaf Fuck off! You're a lying cunt!

Billy Shaf come to the bar with me!

Billy *takes* **Shaf** *by the arm and heads towards the bar.*

Billy What the fuck's up with you? . . . You've been on his case since he got here . . . you really know how to fuck a night up.

Shaf You know fuck all Billy man . . . he's a two-faced cunt . . . a fucking snake . . . if you knew the fucking truth . . . you'd think the same.

Billy What's he done? . . . Why don't you tell me?

Shaf (*hesitates*) Take the whole drinking thing . . . he's been going on like he's a fucking saint and all the time he's just another pisshead.

Billy All he said was that he didn't want a drink.

Shaf It's not just that . . .

Billy What else is there?

Shaf (*hesitates again*) Fuck it . . . just forget about it.

Billy Only if you're going to stop acting like a complete dickhead.

Shaf *just nods,* **Billy** *claps him on the shoulder.*

Billy Order the drinks; I'm just going for a piss.

Billy *heads towards the toilets.* **Dave** *arrives.*

Dave   What can I get you?

Shaf *thinks a moment.*

Shaf   Four tequilas, two pints, a bottle of Bud and double Bacardi and coke . . . make it a triple.

Dave *starts getting the drinks together.*

Dave   How's the game going?

Shaf   Alright.

Dave   What does your mate keep shouting? . . . Poorty something.

Shaf *gives* **Dave** *a confused look.*

Dave   You know when he misses a shot . . . he shouts something, in your language . . . something beginning with pah . . .

Shaf   Oh that . . . poody tie knee.

Dave   Poorty.

Shaf   No . . . poody.

Dave   Poody.

Shaf   Tie.

Dave   Tie.

Shaf   Knee.

Dave   Knee.

Shaf   Poody tie knee.

Dave   Poody tie knee . . . what does it mean?

Shaf   My aunty's fanny.

Dave   Your aunty.

Shaf   No . . . not my fucking aunty . . . his aunty.

Dave   So it's like a swear word.

Shaf   Yeah . . . shall I tell you what . . . shoot another Bacardi in that.

Dave   Are you sure?

Shaf   The lad who's drinking it is a bit of an alkie mate . . . he won't even feel that.

Dave *adds another shot of Bacardi to the glass.*

Dave   So there's a lot riding on this game then.

Shaf   You wouldn't believe.

Dave *puts the drinks on the bar.*

Dave   £18.80 please.

Shaf *hands over a twenty as* **Billy** *returns from the toilet.*

Billy   What the fuck have you ordered?

Shaf   Chill out Bill, it's a pissup isn't it?

Billy   We don't have to do it in one fucking go.

Shaf   This is nowt.

Dave *gives* **Shaf** *his change.*

Billy   It was my round.

Shaf   Get the next one.

The lads get the drinks and head back to the table.

Kamy   I'm not drinking any more of that tequila!

Mo   I don't want any of that shit.

Shaf *puts the drinks down on the table.*

Shaf   Right listen to me . . . before you start bitching about I'm not drinking this or I'm not drinking that . . . we're having a pissup . . . we're celebrating . . . if you don't drink

them then I'm going to neck mine and fuck off somewhere
else . . . now pick up your drinks.

Shaf *picks up his tequila, the other lads hesitate a moment before*
Billy *picks up his shot followed by the other two.*

Mo   What we drinking to?

Kamy   What we always drink to.

Billy   Talub.

The lads touch glasses, neck the tequila, lick salt and suck on the
lemon. Then they all grab their drinks and start to wash it down. **Mo**
takes a huge gulp of his drink and retches, he runs towards the toilet.
Shaf *starts laughing.*

Billy   What the fuck have you put in his drink?

Shaf   Fuck all . . . it's Bacardi.

Kamy *picks up the drink, sniffs it and then takes a sip.*

Kamy (*laughs*)   It's fucking rocket fuel . . . how many did
you put in there?

Billy   You're out of order.

Shaf   It's only a laugh . . . the miserable bastard . . . anyway
he's got some catching up to do.

Billy   You're a fucking prick.

Mo *returns from the toilet wiping his mouth. He is glaring at* **Shaf**.
The lads are trying to keep straight faces.

Billy   You okay Mo?

Mo   Yeah . . . it just went down the wrong way.

Shaf   I'll get you another one if that's too strong for you.

Mo   Fuck you! I'll drink the one I've got.

Kamy   We can wait a bit if you want Mo.

Mo   No, no, I'm alright, I don't want to wait . . . come on whose break is it?

Shaf *picks up a cue and breaks. The first shots are played in silence, there's an atmosphere that* **Billy** *tries to break.*

Billy   When's T's thing?

Kamy   What thing?

Billy   The . . . err . . . is it khatam?

Mo   Yeah, khatam.

Billy   When is it?

Mo   It's in a couple of weeks.

Billy   What's all that about?

Mo   You're praying for the person who's died.

Kamy   You're asking God to forgive him . . .

Billy   Forgive him . . .

Shaf   . . . Are you coming back for it?

Billy   I can't . . . I've got work.

Shaf   It's going to be on a weekend . . . come back up for it . . . it's a good thing.

Kamy   I thought you didn't believe in all that religion.

Shaf   I don't . . . I go round for his mum . . . help out.

Mo   Don't you believe in God? . . . Why doesn't that surprise me.

Shaf   I thought you were doing enough religion for the whole town . . . turns out you're not.

Billy   Shaf . . .

Shaf   No . . . he goes on like he's Mr Islam 2012, when really he's just a pisshead like the rest of us.

Billy Just leave it for fuck's sake.

Shaf Let him explain himself . . . one minute he's first in the queue to Mecca and the next he's in here necking Bacardi . . . what's all that about then?

Mo I've told you I didn't stop drinking because of the religion.

Shaf Fuck off.

Kamy Why did you stop then?

Mo *hesitates.*

Shaf It's all a fucking act.

Mo I don't need a drink to get through the day like you . . .

Kamy You're not on a diet aya?

The lads laugh.

Mo 'Course not . . .

Shaf So why did you stop then?

Billy Did you really stop . . .

Mo Yeah yeah I did . . . only for a while.

Shaf He's full of shit.

Kamy Why have you started again then?

Mo Fucking hell can't a man have a drink?

Billy Only if you tell us why you packed in.

Shaf He's got fuck all to tell.

Kamy Is that right Mo?

Mo I stopped because . . .

Shaf Because he's a hypocrite . . .

Billy Shut up Shaf he was going to tell us there . . . go on Mo.

Mo   I needed to . . .

Kamy   So you didn't want to . . . you had to.

Shaf   Somebody hold a gun to your head . . .

Mo   The doctors told me.

Billy   Doctors?

Mo   I went for fucking IVF.

Billy   You've had IVF?

Mo   Our lass has.

Billy   How did it go?

Mo   No joy.

Billy   Sorry mate.

Mo   There's a couple of clinics in London that are supposed to be very good, if I get this job we'll try them.

Shaf   How long have you been having that?

Mo   If you were ever at home you'd know . . . all the family knows.

Kamy   Did you have to pay for it?

Mo   Yeah.

Kamy   How much?

Mo   Three grand a pop.

Kamy   Fucking hell!

Mo   It's not the money . . . you'd pay anything . . . do anything . . . anything at all . . . you just want it to work . . . it's the waiting that's fucking horrible . . . and then you're devastated when it's a negative result . . . you'd do anything to have kids.

Billy   Mate it will work out for you . . . I'm sure . . . don't worry . . . when you get to London we'll suss these clinics out.

Shaf   Can we concentrate on the game please.

Kamy *takes a shot . . . and misses.*

Kamy   Poody tie knee!

Shaf   You daft bastard it's not your aunty's fault!

Kamy   Shut the fuck up Shaf . . . you sound like one of those old women that come into the shop.

Shaf   Yeah well get used to it . . . because that's what you're going to be doing for the rest of your life.

Billy   Leave him alone Shaf . . . he'll be supplying all the schools in the county soon.

Mo   Yeah and the hospitals . . . what are you going to be doing? . . . driving your taxi.

Shaf   Don't worry about me . . . I'll be sorted soon.

Billy   Come on then Shaf . . . what's this big idea?

Shaf   I'll tell you later.

Kamy   He's full of shit.

Billy   Just tell me now . . . I'm sure nobody is going to nick it.

Mo   There's fuck all to tell.

Billy (*mockingly*)   Come on Shaf it's only the lads . . . you can tell us.

Shaf *hesitates a moment.*

Shaf   Do you know how much money there is in food?

Kamy   You want to open a kebab shop . . . is that your big fucking idea?

Shaf   No! Not a kebab shop . . . a chicken shop.

Billy   Halal chicken . . . like Kamy does.

Shaf   No you fool . . . chicken as in chicken and chips.

Mo   There's already chicken shops . . . loads of them.

Shaf   Not like my chicken shop.

Kamy   What you going to do . . . use lamb?

The lads laugh.

Mo   How's yours going to be different?

Shaf *is ignoring the other lads and pitching his idea at* **Billy**.

Shaf   I'm . . . we, me and you are going to do all sorts of chicken . . . chicken like Kentucky . . . chicken like Nando's . . . chicken tikka . . . chicken salad . . .

Kamy   Yeah we get it . . . it's going to be a chicken shop.

Mo *and* **Kamy** *laugh but* **Shaf** *is ignoring them.*

Shaf   It's going to be fresh and funky . . . sit in or take away . . . everything halal for the fundamentalists . . .

Billy   What you going to do, make me wear a chicken costume?

Shaf   I've done my research . . . everybody loves chicken . . . them Africans . . . West Indians, apney . . . mate we'll make it the place to be . . . wicked music . . . done up proper smart . . . attract the young 'uns . . . we can do barbecued chicken . . . I've even thought of a name . . . Clucking Gorgeous!

Kamy   Fucking Clucking Gorgeous!

Shaf   But if you don't like that we can think of something else . . . I'm telling you Billy we can make some serious cash.

Billy *realises that* **Shaf** *is very serious.*

Billy   Shaf . . . I can't bro . . . I live in London . . . I've got a job.

Shaf (*almost pleading now*)   Please mate . . . we can do this . . . me and you.

Mo   It cost about fifty grand to kit one of those shops out . . . where are you going to get that type of money?

Billy   That's another thing; I haven't got a penny to scratch my arse with.

Shaf   Don't worry about the money . . . I've got the money boxed off.

Mo   Where have you got fifty grand from?

Shaf (*turning on* **Mo**)   None of your business!

Billy   Shaf chill out . . . why me? . . . why now?

Shaf   Look at us . . . what are we doing? . . . At our age we should be getting our shit together . . . this is our chance mate . . . this is our ticket to the big time.

Billy   It's your chance Shaf . . . it's not for me . . . I'll help you all I can.

Shaf   I don't want your help . . . not like that . . . I want you as my partner . . . fuck all can stop us if we're together.

Billy   I can't come back Shaf.

Shaf   Why not . . . what have you got down there that you couldn't have up here . . . this isn't about Sharon is it . . . you're not back with that cunt?

Billy (*annoyed*)   It's fuck all to do with Sharon . . . I've told you I haven't seen her in years.

Shaf   But I don't understand it Bill . . . why don't you want to do it . . . we can set ourselves up . . . what's stopping you doing that?

Mo   Because he doesn't want to.

Shaf   You mean because you don't want him to . . . you want him to stay in London so he can help you.

Mo   I haven't even got the job yet.

Shaf   You want him to struggle . . . you want to lord it over him . . . like you do with the rest of us.

Mo   What the fuck are you going on about? . . . You don't know what you're talking about.

Billy   Will you just shut up! I don't need this . . . not tonight . . . I came here to chill out!

The lads are stunned by **Billy**'s *outburst.*

Kamy   Come on lads let's forget about it . . . let's play. Whose shot is it?

Billy   It's mine.

The game resumes, there is a tension.

Shaf   All I'm saying Billy is will you think about it?

Kamy   Just fucking leave it Shaf.

Mo   He can't can he.

Billy   Fuck this, I need a piss.

Billy *leaves.*

Kamy   Why are you doing his head in for Shaf?

Shaf   I'm trying to help him . . . sort his future out for him . . . I don't see you two doing anything for him.

Mo   I don't think you should mention it again.

Shaf   Why doesn't that surprise me.

Mo   Fuck you!

Kamy   Leave it out lads . . .

Shaf   It's fuck all to do with you.

Kamy   Why isn't it . . . he's my mate as well.

Mo   He doesn't give a fuck about Billy . . . it's what's good for him.

Shaf   Yeah and you do care about him . . . if you did you snake . . . you wouldn't have done that.

Mo   What have I supposed to have done?

Shaf   I'll tell you what you did . . .

Kamy   Behave lads he's coming back.

The lads fall silent as **Billy** *goes to the bar, orders some drinks and* **Dave** *indicates he'll bring them to the table.* **Billy** *comes back to the table.*

Billy   Listen Shaf, the reason I can't come back is that I went to my mum and dad's today . . . it didn't go well.

Kamy   What happened?

Billy   It was a bit mad.

Mo   Who was there, both of them?

Billy   Just Mum.

Shaf   What did she say?

Billy   I knocked on the door and Mum opened it . . . she just started crying . . . and then she started kissing me, kissing my hands, my eyes, my face . . . it was mad . . . and I started crying . . . and then . . . and then she said, 'My son's dead' and she shut the door on me.

Kamy   Fucking hell.

Shaf   What did you do?

Billy   What could I do?

Shaf   Didn't you knock on the door again?

Billy   How could I knock on the door after that?

Mo   I'm sorry mate.

Shaf   We can go back round tomorrow.

Billy   I'm not going back round.

Shaf   What do you mean you're not going back round? . . .
You've done the hardest part . . . you've made contact.

Billy   I'm dead to them.

Shaf   Billy don't leave it at that . . . go back round.

Billy   I can't.

Shaf   Of course you can.

Billy   I can't . . . and I can't come back here . . . not
permanently . . . I don't want to be avoiding them all the
time . . . I don't want people going round telling them that
I'm in town.

Shaf   It won't be like that . . . you need to go round and sort
it out.

Billy   No.

Shaf   Are you fucking stupid!

Mo   Leave him alone . . . Billy just do what you think's best.

Billy   I will.

Shaf   You're making a mistake Billy . . . you've got to
strike whilst the iron is hot . . . go back round . . . I'll come
with you.

Kamy   What did your dad say?

Billy   He wasn't there.

Kamy   It might be worth seeing what he says.

Billy   He's just going to say what my mum said.

Shaf   You don't know that.

Billy   Look I've told you why I aren't coming back . . . let's just leave it at that.

Shaf   But you can't just leave it like that . . . they're your mum and dad.

Kamy   You should try again you know mate.

Billy   Maybe I will . . . next time I come up.

Dave *brings the drinks over and puts them on the table. When he's left, the lads pick up the drinks.*

Shaf   To coming home.

Kamy   Coming home.

Mo *and* **Billy** *stay silent, they touch glasses and neck the shots.*

Billy   Come on then whose shot is it?

Kamy   Mine.

The game resumes.

Shaf   How come now Billy?

Billy   What?

Shaf   Why did you decide to go round now?

Mo   Can't you just fucking leave it.

Billy   It's alright Mo . . . it was when I was at the cemetery today . . . I just thought the next time I come it could be Mum or Dad in here . . . so I plucked up the courage and went round.

Shaf   And that's the first time you thought about it?

Billy   No . . . I've been thinking about it since me and Sharon split up.

Kamy   Have you seen her since?

Billy   No . . . never.

Kamy   Haven't even talked to her?

Billy   No.

Shaf   She was a dodgy bastard.

Mo   Let's just talk about something else.

Shaf   Why do you want to talk about something else?

Mo   I don't, it's for Billy, he doesn't want to talk about it.

Shaf   He's a grown man, he can talk about what he wants.

Mo   You're just doing his head in.

Shaf   You mean you don't want to talk about it?

Mo   What the fuck have I got to do with anything?

Shaf   You've got everything to do with it . . . you two-faced cunt!

Mo   Fuck you!

Billy   What the fuck's up with you two?

Shaf   Ask him.

Mo   I don't know what the prick's going on about.

Shaf   Don't you.

Billy   Shaf! Fucking behave!

Shaf *is silent, he can't believe that* **Billy** *is taking* **Mo***'s side.*

Shaf   Fuck that, I want more drink.

He heads to the bar; there is a moment's silence.

Mo   Listen Billy . . . if you don't want to come back . . . that's alright . . . don't let that knobhead pressure you . . . wait until I come to London and we can take it from there.

Billy   That's what I'm going to do.

Kamy   Mo . . .

Billy   He's right Kamy . . . I don't want to rush into things.

Mo   You know I'm right . . . when I get down there we can sit and sort out the right way to do things.

Shaf *returns from the bar, he is in a foul mood.*

Mo   You know I'm right Billy.

Shaf *puts tequilas on the table.*

Kamy   I don't think I can handle any more of them.

Shaf   If you don't want it don't have it, I'll drink the fucking thing.

Shaf *picks up his drink and downs it, followed by* **Billy***, then* **Mo** *and reluctantly* **Kamy***.*

Shaf   Whose shot is it?

Mo   Mine.

Shaf   Well get a fucking move on then.

Lights fade.

Scene Four

Kamy *is about to take a shot, the black ball sits over the pocket . . . unmissable. As he lines up the shot his phone starts to ring. He takes the phone from his pocket and looks at it.*

Kamy   Withheld number . . . fucking hate that.

The phone stops ringing and he returns it to his pocket . . . he lines up the shot again.

Mo   Don't be missing this Kamy . . . it's for the championship.

Kamy   Don't worry, I won't.

Mo   I'm just saying . . . pressure.

Shaf   We don't need a running fucking commentary . . . don't be missing Kamy.

Just as **Kamy** *is about to take the shot his phone starts ringing again. He stops and takes out the phone.*

Kamy   What the fuck . . . why do people do that?

Shaf   Just answer the fucking thing and tell whoever it is to fuck off.

Kamy   Hello . . . who's this? . . . No you tell me who this is . . . listen fuck face you tell me who you are . . . you phoned me . . . what missed calls? . . . I haven't gave anybody a missed call . . . either tell me who you are or fuck off . . .

Shaf *realises who is on the phone and snatches it from* **Kamy***.*

Shaf   Is that Ditta . . .

The other guys are stunned to hear this name.

Shaf   . . . yeah yeah we still on . . . yeah I've got it . . . doesn't matter where . . . have you got what I need? . . . it doesn't matter who that was . . . let's just get this done . . . tomorrow . . . okay I'll see you there . . .

He hangs up and hands the phone back to **Kamy** *. . . who is reluctant to take it.*

Kamy   What the fuck! What you doing phoning nutters like that off my phone?

Shaf   Calm down.

Kamy   Don't tell me to calm down . . . don't you fucking dare tell me to calm down . . . that psycho gets people shot!

Shaf   Does he fuck . . . they're just rumours.

Kamy   They're not rumours . . . he had Sajjy Iqbal shot . . .

Billy   Even if they're rumours, why are you getting mixed up with those sorts of people you knobhead?

Shaf   It's alright Billy man . . . I know what I'm doing.

Mo   That's where the fifty grand's coming from Billy.

Shaf *turns on* **Mo**.

Shaf   It's fuck all to do with you!

Mo   I'm glad I've got fuck all to do with it.

Kamy   I told him to fuck off.

Mo   Sajjy Iqbal told him to fuck off and look what happened to him.

Billy   Shaf man . . .

Kamy   Fuck . . . fuck fuck fuck.

Shaf   Calm down you pussy . . . just take your shot.

Kamy   Fuck you . . . I need a drink.

Mo   I'll come with you.

Mo *and* **Kamy** *head to the bar.*

Billy   What the fuck you doing you prick?

Shaf   It's under control Billy . . . I need you to come back.

Billy   No!

Shaf   Please . . . you're my best mate . . . I need you.

Billy   Shaf, shut up man.

Shaf   You know when you said I was . . .

Billy   Don't Shaf . . .

Shaf   I need you . . .

Billy   No.

Shaf   Please Billy.

Billy   I can't . . .

Shaf   For me . . .

Billy   It's not happening . . .

Shaf   I'll do all the work . . .

Billy   I said no . . .

Shaf   Billy please come back . . .

Billy   I can't . . . haven't you been listening to what I've been telling you?

Shaf   Please . . . do you want me to beg you . . . I'll beg if that's what it takes . . .

Billy   Don't be fucking stupid.

Shaf   Why then?

Billy *notices the other two coming back from the bar . . . he just shakes his head . . .* **Shaf** *is deflated. The lads put the drinks on the table.*

Billy   Drink these and we'll get this game finished.

The lads drink their drinks . . . **Kamy** *reluctantly picks the cue up . . . he takes the shot and . . . misses.*

Shaf   How the fuck did you miss that you fucking prick!

Kamy   Shut the fuck up! Just shut the fuck up!

Shaf   What do you mean shut up! It was sat over the pocket . . . a fucking blind man could have potted that!

Kamy   I didn't mean to miss did I . . . I didn't think 'fuck this I'm going to miss' and lose the game did I!

Mo   Two shots on the black.

Shaf   Is it fuck! One shot on the black!

Mo   It's two.

Shaf   We're not playing them rules . . . it's one.

Mo   It's two.

Billy   It's one Mo.

Mo (*hesitates*)   Fair enough . . . but I'm sure it's two.

Mo *takes aim and pots the ball . . . he starts celebrating . . .* **Shaf** *kicks a stool over . . .* **Mo** *suddenly stops and turns to* **Kamy** *and* **Shaf.**

Mo   Put the T-shirt on.

Shaf (*defiant*)   I'm not putting it on.

Mo   You have to put it on.

Shaf   Why don't you make me.

Mo   Put the fucking T-shirt on!

Shaf   Like I said big man . . . why don't you make me?

Billy   Just leave the fucking T-shirts.

Mo   No! we're not leaving the T-shirts . . . this fucker has to put one on . . . that's what we play for . . . and he lost so he has to put it on.

Shaf   There's not a man in this town that can make me put that T-shirt on.

Billy   Fucking hell just forget about the fucking T-shirts . . . it was a stupid idea anyway . . . fucking T-shirts.

Kamy   It wasn't a stupid idea . . . we always put the T-shirts on . . . you're only saying it's stupid because it's my idea.

Shaf   Well if you think it's a good idea . . . you put one on then daft lad.

Kamy   Fuck you I will.

Kamy *goes to the carrier bag and puts a T-shirt on . . . it bears the legend* 'I am a big fucking loser'. **Shaf** *just shakes his head in contempt.*

Mo   Right, now I want him to put one on.

Shaf   Fuck you.

Shaf *steps up . . . it looks like it's going to kick off.*

Kamy   Just put the T-shirt on.

Shaf If you're stupid enough to put one on go for it . . . you're the prick that cost us the game anyway.

Kamy I only got beat because I had you on my side.

Shaf You what! You missed a fucking sitter!

Kamy You've been phoning gangsters off my phone.

Shaf What the fuck has that got to do with anything?

Kamy I never get beat when I'm playing with that cue.

Shaf That fucking cue . . . shall I tell you something about that cue . . .

Billy Don't Shaf . . .

Shaf Fuck him . . . he needs to know the truth . . . that isn't Stephen Hendry's cue you knobhead . . .

Billy Shaf!

Shaf He found it in a fucking skip . . . do you think if it was Stephen Hendry's he'd of gave it to you . . .

Kamy You're a fucking liar!

Shaf Ask these . . . they know the truth . . .

Kamy Billy . . .

Billy What does it matter where he got it . . . he gave it to you didn't he?

Kamy *is crestfallen . . . he slumps into a chair.*

Kamy He thought I was an idiot . . . you all did . . . still do . . .

Billy It's not like that Kamy.

Shaf It is.

Billy Shut the fuck up Shaf! . . . look Kamy it doesn't matter what he said . . . he wanted you to have the cue . . . T was a good lad . . . he didn't think you were an idiot . . . none of us do.

Kamy Don't Billy . . . I know, alright . . . do you think I didn't know when you used to send me to the shops like a skivvy . . . or take the piss . . . do you think I was that thick that I didn't even realise what you were doing. I knew . . . I've always known . . . but I put up with it . . . because I wanted to be like you lot . . . I wanted to be your mate . . . a proper mate . . .

Shaf If you've known for so long why didn't you say anything eh?

Kamy Because you were my mates . . . I loved you . . . I thought you'd change . . .

Billy Kamy man . . .

Shaf Well you were fucking wrong weren't you?

Kamy I know that now.

Shaf Took your fucking time.

Kamy Fuck you! I know who I am . . . what I am . . . do you know what you are? . . . Who you are? . . . You're fuck all . . . all of you . . . fuck all . . . I can't believe I wanted to be like you lot . . . you're all full of shit . . . T told me . . . and I thought he was lying . . . but it turns out he wasn't.

Billy What did T say?

Kamy The truth for once . . . do you want the truth Billy?

Billy *is silent.*

Shaf Shut up Kamy . . .

Kamy What's the matter Shaf . . . you said I needed to know the truth . . . don't you think Billy should know the truth? . . . What about you Mo? . . . Do you think Billy should know the truth?

Mo *is silent.*

Kamy   You might want to sit down Billy.

Mo *and* **Shaf** *are looking nervous . . .* **Billy** *is confused.*

Billy   What's going on?

Kamy   T didn't die of an overdose Billy . . . he killed himself . . . put a rope around his neck and hung himself.

Billy   What?

Kamy   He hung himself Billy.

Billy   What do you mean he hung himself?

Kamy   Committed suicide.

Billy *sits down.*

Shaf   Get the fuck out of here!

Kamy   I'm going.

Shaf   You're lucky I don't give you a bat!

Kamy   You're good at that aren't you? . . . And what are you going to do Mo? . . . are you going to fuck me?

Kamy *grabs his coat and heads for the door . . . he looks back at the lads and shakes his head . . .*

Kamy   Fucking pricks.

. . . and leaves . . . there is silence . . . finally **Shaf** *speaks.*

Shaf   Are you alright Billy?

Billy *looks up.*

Billy   He's lying isn't he?

Mo   Billy . . .

Billy   Tell me he's lying . . . that can't be true . . . I'm not having any of it . . .

Shaf   Billy . . .

Billy Fuck that I know he's lying . . . T would never do that . . . that wasn't his style . . . he was a fucking gadgy . . . heart of a lion . . . he's a cheeky cunt that Kamy . . . wait till I see him . . . cheeky fucker . . . my mate T would never do anything like that . . . never!

The other two are silent.

Billy Why didn't you two stop him saying that? . . . That's a fucking out of order thing to say . . . fuck that . . . I'm going to tell him . . .

Billy *gets up and tries to head to the door . . .* **Shaf** *stops him.*

Shaf Sit down Billy . . .

Billy No fuck him . . . who the fuck does Kamy he think he is? . . . Well I'll show that fucker . . . I'll kick his fucking head in saying shit like that . . . I'll put a fucking glass in his face!

Shaf Billy sit down.

He forces **Billy** *into a chair . . .* **Billy** *starts crying.*

Billy Why didn't you stop him? . . . Why the fuck didn't you stop him saying that!

Shaf Do you want some water?

Billy No! . . . I want you to tell me he's full of shit.

Shaf *is silent.*

Billy You tell me Mo.

Mo *is silent.*

Billy Say something then.

Mo Sorry Billy.

Billy I don't want to hear sorry . . . sorry's no good to me . . .

Shaf *heads to the bar . . .* **Mo** *watches him go and then crouches beside* **Billy**.

Mo   There was nothing anybody could have done Billy . . .
he was in a bad way . . . it's this town . . . it's poison . . . it
just fucking grinds you down mate . . . you're better off out
of here . . . we all are . . . and that fucker trying to get you
mixed up with the people responsible for what happened to
T . . . he's out of order . . .

Billy   Who was responsible . . . what do you mean?

Shaf *returns with a glass of water.*

Shaf   Here.

He hands the water to **Billy** . . . *who drinks it in big gulps.*

Billy   What happened . . .?

Shaf   When?

Billy   What happened to my mate!

Shaf   He's fucking dead, what more do you want to know?
. . . Isn't that enough?

Billy   What aren't you telling me . . .?

Shaf   What do you mean by that . . .?

Mo *walks away.*

Billy   Why didn't somebody tell me?

Shaf   Because nobody knew where you were . . . Billy stop
it . . .

Billy   I can't.

Shaf   There was an autopsy.

Billy   Those fuckers will say anything.

Shaf   No they don't . . . I'll get all the paperwork from his
mum . . . you can see for yourself.

Billy   Now?

Shaf Not now . . . tomorrow . . . when you come back . . . if you come back I'll get you everything you need . . . get you all the answers.

Mo *returns.*

Billy Can you do that?

Shaf I'll try.

Billy Promise?

Shaf I swear down.

Mo Promise what?

Shaf None of your business.

Billy Shaf's going to find out what really happened.

Mo Billy man . . . listen to what he's saying to you . . . what the fuck can he do? . . . He's telling you fucking lies again.

Shaf I can get him all the paperwork from T's mum alright . . . he can see for himself. I'm not telling him any lies . . . not like fucking you.

Mo You just conveniently forget to tell the truth don't you.

Shaf Fuck you.

Mo You didn't tell Billy about T . . .

Shaf And you did . . .

Mo You didn't tell him about fucking Ditta and how you're going to make him sell drugs for a living . . .

Shaf What the fuck are you going on about? . . .

Mo You haven't told anybody about your pregnant white slut!

Shaf *is stunned.*

Mo Yeah you haven't told anybody about that have you? . . . You haven't told your mum . . . your wife . . . your five fucking kids . . . you tried to keep that dirty little secret . . . but I know . . . I know about your dirty white slut . . . and when your white slut is pushing your bastard child about in a pram the whole fucking town's going to know . . . you're a fucking embarrassment . . . and your white slut will be an embarrassment . . .

Shaf Stop calling her a slut . . . she's not a slut.

Mo (*laughing*) I don't fucking believe it . . . he's in love with her . . . that's just typical . . . actually you'll make the perfect couple . . . the fuck-up loser and the white slut . . .

Shaf *punches* **Mo***, knocking him flat, his head banging off the floor. He stands over him.*

Shaf I said don't call her a slut.

Mo Fuck . . . you can't do that.

Mo *tries to get up.* **Shaf** *pushes him back down.*

Shaf Did you think Sharon was a slut?

Mo What the fuck are you going on about?

Shaf You know what I'm going on about.

Mo *feels the back of his head . . . it's bleeding.*

Mo I need to go to the hospital . . .

Shaf You're going nowhere . . . who have you told that you were shagging Sharon eh . . .

Billy Shaf?

Mo You're a lying bastard!

Shaf He was Billy . . . you fucking were . . . don't fucking deny it . . . T told me . . .

Mo You're only saying T because he's not here to say different . . .

Shaf It is fucking true . . . T gave me all the details.

Mo   What the fuck did he know . . . he was out of his tree all the time.

Shaf   Swear down then . . . swear that you'll never have kids if what I'm saying is true.

Mo   What the fuck . . . I'm not fucking seven . . . it's all mumbo jumbo . . .

Shaf   If it's all mumbo jumbo then it won't be a problem saying it . . .

Mo *is looking uncomfortable . . . he can't look the lads in the eye . . . he hesitates a moment too long.*

Billy   Just say it Mo . . . say it and I won't believe a word he's saying . . .

Mo *is silent.*

Shaf   I told you Billy he's a fucking snake . . .

Billy   Let him get up.

Shaf *takes a step back and* **Mo** *reluctantly stands . . .* **Billy** *goes and sits down, the boys are silent.*

Mo   What was so good about T . . . why did you all think he was something special . . . he wasn't . . . I was as good as him . . . but you never seen that did you . . . it was all about T . . . you weren't fair with me . . . especially you Billy . . . you weren't fair.

Mo *leaves and the lads are silent . . . eventually* **Billy** *speaks.*

Billy   Did you see T?

Shaf   What?

Billy   Did you see T before he died?

Shaf   A couple of weeks before.

Billy   What did he say?

Shaf   I can't remember . . . loads of things.

Billy Like what . . . did he say anything about me?

Shaf I don't fucking know . . . he said loads of things . . . he was a fucking smackhead.

Billy He was our mate!

Shaf Our mate the smackhead.

Billy Don't fucking call him that!

Shaf What do you want me to call him?

Billy I want you to call him our mate . . . I want you to say he was a top fucking bloke . . . that he was unlucky . . . that he didn't fucking kill himself . . . that's what I want you to say!

Shaf I can't.

Billy Yes you can! You can say all sorts of other bullshit, why can't you say that! Say it! Fucking say it!

Shaf *is silent.*

Billy You're a fucking cunt!

Shaf We're all cunts.

Billy T wasn't.

Shaf You're wrong.

Billy How would you fucking know?

Shaf Because I was here!

The lads are silent.

Billy He told me to go.

Shaf T?

Billy He was the one that said I should fuck off . . . with Sharon.

Shaf Yeah he was all fucking heart.

Billy *throws* **Shaf** *a sharp look.*

Billy   What's your fucking problem eh . . . what have you got against him?

Shaf *retrieves the bag from under the table, unzips it and shows* **Billy** *the contents.*

Billy   What the fuck's that?

Shaf   Ten £10,000 kilos.

Billy   Fucking drugs!

Shaf   Keep your voice you down you prick!

Billy   What the fuck are you doing with them?

Shaf   I found them.

Billy   Just get rid of it.

Shaf   I'm going to.

Billy   No I mean bin it.

Shaf   Fuck off . . . I'll never get another chance like this . . . it's alright for you . . . but it's a hundred grand Billy . . . where are lads like us going to get a hundred grand from? . . . We can set up the shop and have money in the bank.

Billy   I'm not going to do it.

Shaf   Why not?

Billy   You shouldn't do it.

Shaf   That's easy for you to say.

Billy   Me! You haven't got a fucking clue!

Shaf   It's my ticket Billy . . . do you think everybody's nice? . . . Do you think people give a fuck where your money comes from? . . . Do they fuck! They're only bothered about whether you've got it or not . . . that mosque's full of drug dealers . . . VAT fraudsters . . . dodgy fuckers . . . everybody knows . . . they still there shaking their hands . . .

licking their arses . . . so why can't I make my future? . . .
Why shouldn't I set myself up? . . . They have kids to white
women . . . no fuckers say anything to them . . . give me one
good reason why I shouldn't do this.

Billy   Because drugs killed T!

Shaf   T killed T!

Billy   Everything killed T . . . we killed T.

Shaf   Stop making excuses for him.

Billy   It's not an excuse.

Shaf   He was weak . . . he was a liar . . . he wasn't the person
he made out he was . . . that person would never have done
that to themselves . . . T was full of shit.

Billy   Fuck you! You're out of fucking order!

Shaf   It's true . . . he said he was my mate . . . a mate would
never have let me down like that.

Billy   It's always got to be about you doesn't it?

Shaf   I'm sick of thinking of others.

Billy   When have you ever thought of others?

Shaf   When I married the girl they wanted me to marry
. . . when I had the kids they wanted me to have . . . when I
stayed in this shit hole like they wanted me to . . . my whole
life's been about what other people want . . . not what I want
. . . well fuck that Billy . . . I'm getting what's mine . . . I've
got fuck all . . .

Billy   I've got fuck all.

Shaf   You've got freedom.

Billy   It's not what it's made out to be.

Shaf   I'm in jail Bill . . . no walls but loads of fucking guards
. . . an open fucking prison . . . you live in London . . . you've
got the easy life . . .

Billy   You don't know what it's like.

Shaf   What is it like? . . . Tell me . . . explain to thick Shaf
. . . go on explain . . . you've always did what you wanted
. . . what was good for you . . . in fact you're the fucker that's
never thought of anybody else . . . not me.

Billy *is silent a moment.*

Billy   Yeah you're right I did always think of myself . . . I
did always do what was good for me . . . and where has it
got me . . . you have a mother that loves you . . . I don't . . .
you have people who care for you . . . I don't . . . do you
know what it feels like to abandon your parents . . . do you
think that's freedom . . . I was their light . . . that's what they
used to call me, their light . . . I snubbed that out . . . broke
their hearts . . . left them with nothing . . . is that what you
want . . . you're fucking welcome to it . . . have it . . . please
just take it . . . because it's doing my fucking head in . . . you
call what I've got freedom . . . my prison is in my head . . .
in my fucking heart . . . in fucking London . . . and all the
money in the world won't . . . can't get me out of that . . . and
tonight . . . tonight is just another lock on my cell door so
don't stand there and tell me how fucking hard it is for you!

Shaf   Well fucking change it then . . . do something about it
. . . don't be a pussy like T was! . . . fucking wanker wouldn't
even fight back . . . just laid there crying like a fucking
girl . . . (*Mimics a weak T.*) don't Shaf . . . stop it Shaf . . .
you're out of order Shaf . . . FUCKING STAND UP! . . .
FIGHT . . . PUNCH ME . . . KICK ME . . . DO FUCKING
SOMETHING!

Shaf *hasn't realised but there are tears streaming down his face . . .*
Billy *is just staring at him.*

Shaf   . . . What the fuck are you looking at? . . . Yeah I
battered the daft cunt! Fucking smackhead thief . . . nicking
his mum's gold . . . fucker deserved it . . . fucking pussy . . .
nobody does that to me . . .

Billy   Are you going to batter me as well?

Shaf   What the fuck for?

Billy   I'm weak . . . I'm a pussy like T.

Shaf   You're fuck all like him . . . I can trust you.

Billy   T trusted me . . .

Shaf   Yeah and you were there for him . . . like I want you to be there for me . . . come on Billy you'd do it for T . . . Why won't you do it for me?

Billy   He's dead . . . how was I there for him?

Shaf   There was nothing you could have done about that.

Billy   Wasn't there?

Shaf   No there wasn't.

Billy   If I sent you a text message . . . and it said 'HELP' but then it had a lol on the end what would you think?

Shaf   I'd think you were fucking about.

Billy   Exactly . . . because lol . . . lol means laugh out loud doesn't it . . . it means you're not serious . . . that you're having a laugh . . .

Shaf   Who sent you that?

Billy   You can't take it seriously . . . if it's serious then you don't put lol on the end do you?

Shaf   It was T wasn't it?

Billy   I thought he was joking . . . he was always fucking about like that . . . you wouldn't have taken that seriously would you.

Shaf   When?

Billy   I mean if you're in need of help . . . then you make sure the next man knows . . . why the fuck would you put lol on the end eh . . . what type of fool does that?

Shaf   Why didn't you come back?

Billy   I didn't tell him that Sharon had left me . . .
pretended everything was fine . . . even when I was at my
lowest . . .

Shaf   We were your mates . . . he was your mate.

Billy   The mates that I fucked off . . . how could I tell you
the state I was in . . . you would have said all the right things
. . . but I would have seen it in your eyes . . . I would have
been able to tell what you were thinking . . . and it's the same
now . . . I'll still see it . . . get rid of that bag Shaf . . .

Shaf   You made your choices . . . T made his . . . I'm going
to make mine.

The boys are silent.

Billy   I need to go.

Shaf   Where?

Billy   I don't know.

Shaf   Okay.

Billy *gets up . . . he notices the cue on the table.*

Billy   Can I have this?

Shaf   Not mine to give away.

Billy *very carefully dismantles the cue and puts it in the case. He
looks around the room and then goes over to* **Shaf***.*

Billy   I'll be seeing you some time.

Shaf   You will.

Billy *leaves.* **Shaf** *sits at the table and watches* **Billy** *go.* **Dave**
comes over and starts to collect the glasses.

Dave   He did score a screamer.

Shaf   Who?

Dave   Gary Lineker.

Shaf   When?

Dave   Against Man United . . . I think it was 1989 . . . he was playing for Spurs.

Shaf   No shit.

Dave   No shit . . . he's still a cunt.

Shaf   Isn't he just.

The End.

Printed in the USA
CPSIA information can be obtained
at www.ICGtesting.com
LVHW020930171024
794056LV00003B/700

9 781408 172551